Ghost in the Guitar

PAUL SHIPTON

Level 3

Series Editors: Andy Hopkins and Jocelyn Potter

Pearson Education Limited
Edinburgh Gate, Harlow,
Essex CM20 2JE, England
and Associated Companies throughout the world.

ISBN: 978-1-4058-8184-5

First published 2000
This edition first published 2008

7

Text Copyright © Paul Shipton 2008
Illustrations by Derek Lockhart

Typeset by Graphicraft Ltd, Hong Kong
Set in 11/14pt Bembo
Printed in China
SWTC/07

Published by Pearson Education Ltd

Every effort has been made to trace the copyright holders and we apologise in advance
for any unintentional omissions. We would be pleased to insert the appropriate
acknowledgement in any subsequent edition of this publication.

For a complete list of the titles available in the Pearson English Readers series, please
visit www.pearsonenglishreaders.com. Alternatively, write to your local Pearson Education
office or to Pearson English Readers Marketing Department, Pearson Education,
Edinburgh Gate, Harlow, Essex CM20 2JE, England.

Contents

Introduction

'Let's go to another shop, Tom,' I said. But Tom didn't move. I looked at him. That guitar seemed really good there in his hands. I don't know why. Tom looked like a star. A great star!

Suddenly Tom smiled. I can't explain it, but it wasn't his usual nice smile. This smile was different. It was cold. For a second, I was afraid and I stepped back.

'Don't be silly!' I told myself. I looked again, and Tom's happy smile was back on his face. It went from ear to ear.

'I want this guitar, Katy,' he said.

Katy and her boyfriend Tom are happy in their band, Steel City. They both want to be famous. But then Tom gets a new guitar and the trouble begins. Why can he suddenly play so well? And why is he always so angry? When Katy discovers the secret of the guitar, she is very afraid. She must race against time to save her boyfriend's life. But will she be too late?

Paul Shipton has been a teacher and an editor, but now he stays at home and writes. He has written over a hundred books, mostly for younger people.

Paul Shipton lived in the United States for a long time, but now he lives in Cambridge, in the UK, with his wife and two daughters.

Chapter 1   The Accident

The hands of the factory clock moved slowly. I watched them all day. It seemed a long time until six o'clock.

I was working in an electronics factory. It was my first job, and it was boring. Every day was exactly the same, but it didn't matter to me. The work was easy and I just dreamed all day. I dreamed about being a pop star. I always wanted to be a star, even when I was little. I wanted to play in concerts all over the world. I wanted to be on TV. I wanted to be rich and famous!

Perhaps it was a silly dream, but it wasn't impossible. I was in a band. Three of my friends and I were in it. We were still at school when we started. I played the electric piano and I wrote some of our songs too. Our band was called Steel City. It's a great name for a band, isn't it? (It didn't really mean anything, but we all liked it.)

Finally, six o'clock arrived. Another day was finished. I picked up my bag quickly and ran to the door. I was the first person outside.

I looked around for Tom. He usually met me after work. He was waiting in a car on the other side of the road. It was his father's car. Tom borrowed it so we could drive to gigs. I climbed in next to him.

Tom smiled. 'Hi, Katy,' he said. Most people called me Katherine, but Tom always called me Katy. I liked that.

'How was work?' he asked.

'Boring, thanks!' I said. 'And yours?'

'Mine was boring too!' he laughed. Tom worked in a supermarket. But he was just like me: his job wasn't important to him. He only thought about one thing – Steel City! He was our guitarist. In fact, Steel City was his idea from the start.

I gave him a kiss. (Tom was my boyfriend, too.) He started the car.

'What time are we playing tonight?' I asked. We had a gig that evening in a pub called the King's Arms.

'Eight o'clock,' answered Tom. 'I'll get Aruna first. Then we can go straight to the pub.'

Aruna played bass guitar in the band and she was our singer too. The other person in Steel City was Danny. He was our drummer. His drums were too big to put in a car, so he borrowed his brother's van for gigs.

'It's going to be a good gig tonight,' said Tom with a big smile. I had to laugh. He said the same thing every time. We drove across town to Aruna's house.

♦

Two hours later, we were standing on a small stage in the King's Arms. The pub was crowded, and I was feeling nervous. This was our first time in this pub. I didn't know anyone in the crowd.

The pub owner walked to the microphone. 'Tonight I'm pleased to introduce an exciting new band. Here they are...' He looked at a piece of paper and read our band's name. 'Steel City!'

'One, two, three, four,' counted Danny. Then we started to play. I stopped feeling nervous immediately. Usually I'm a shy person, but I felt great now. I always felt great when I was playing in the band!

The gig was OK. Aruna and Danny were great on bass and drums. Aruna forgot the words to one of my new songs, but it didn't really matter. I was having a good time.

But then there was Tom... He probably played better than usual. He just wasn't a very good guitarist. His musical ideas were good, but not all of those ideas reached his hands or his guitar. He made a few mistakes in every song.

While we played, the crowd didn't stand up. They didn't sing or dance. Some people didn't listen to us at all – they sat and talked all the time. I tried not to notice them. I closed my eyes as I played. In my mind, we weren't in this little pub. No, we were playing in front of thousands of people. They were all wearing STEEL CITY T-shirts.

I opened my eyes and looked at the crowd in the King's Arms. Some of them were enjoying the music, but some of them seemed bored.

'Don't worry,' I told myself. 'We will be stars one day!'

After the gig, we had to carry all our things to Danny's van. Life in a band isn't always easy! The drums were the hardest. Usually we all helped Danny with them first. Then we had a rest. We sat in the room at the back of the pub.

'What time is it?' Tom asked.

Danny looked at his watch. 'Half past ten.'

'Quick!' Tom shouted. 'We've got to listen to the radio.'

'Why?' asked Aruna.

'It's a surprise,' smiled Tom. He rested his guitar against the wall. Then he turned on a small radio in the corner of the room.

We heard the end of a song, and the man on the radio started talking.

'This is it!' said Tom.

'And now it's the time that you're all waiting for,' said the man on the radio. 'It's time for news about this year's Battle of the Bands competition.'

My mouth opened in surprise. We all knew about the Battle of the Bands. It was a big competition for bands in our area. Every year the winners of the competition made a CD at a local record company.

I looked at Tom. 'You didn't . . .'

'Yes,' said Tom, 'I sent a cassette of our songs to the radio station. Perhaps they'll choose us!'

I had to smile. Tom wasn't the best guitarist in the world, but he always had a lot of good ideas.

The man on the radio was saying, 'The competition will be at the City Arena on Saturday the tenth.'

'That's next weekend!' said Aruna. 'It doesn't give us much time. We need to practise.'

All four of us sat there without speaking. We were all thinking the same thing. Steel City, playing in front of a big crowd! I moved closer to the radio. I was excited, but I was nervous too.

'Here are the lucky bands who will be in this year's competition,' said the man on the radio. He started to read a list of names. I closed my eyes and said to myself, 'Steel City, Steel City, Steel City. . .' But I didn't hear our band's name.

Then suddenly the man said, 'And finally, the last band in this year's competition is . . .' We all looked at the radio.

'. . . Steel City!'

'Yes!' shouted Danny. Aruna and Tom started laughing. It was like a dream. I couldn't believe it! We were in the Battle of the Bands!

I wanted to give Tom a big kiss, so I jumped up. I didn't see

Tom's guitar. My leg hit it. I reached out my hand but I was too slow. The guitar fell and hit the floor with a terrible noise.

'Is it OK?' I asked nervously.

Tom didn't say anything. He was looking down at the guitar.

'Perhaps someone can repair it?' suggested Aruna.

Tom picked up the guitar carefully. 'No,' he said softly. 'The neck is completely broken.'

'I'm sorry, Tom,' I said. There were tears in my eyes.

Tom's eyes were sad, but he still smiled at me.

'Don't worry,' he said kindly. 'It was an accident, Katy.' Tom was the nicest person in the world. 'But,' he added, 'I need a new guitar now.'

It was true. We couldn't play in the competition without a guitarist. There was just one small problem – how could we pay for it?

Chapter 2   The New Guitar

I arrived home late that night. Mum and Dad were asleep, but my sister Rachel wasn't in bed yet. I knew what I had to do. I climbed the stairs and knocked on her door.

'Come in,' she said.

Rachel was sitting at her desk and studying. Some music was playing softly on her CD player. Mozart? I wasn't sure. There were history books on the desk in front of my sister. History was her favourite subject. She wanted to go to university the next year to study history. She wanted to become a teacher.

Rachel looked up from her book. 'What do you want?' she asked. Rachel and I didn't spend much time together. Don't worry – I didn't hate her and she didn't hate me. We were just interested in different things.

'Could you lend me some money?' I asked her. Rachel always

had plenty of money. She worked in a shop every Saturday and she saved every penny.

My younger sister just looked at me. I waited.

'It's for your pop band, isn't it?' she asked at last.

In Rachel's opinion, it was silly that I played in the band. In fact, all pop music was silly. She agreed with my parents. They wanted me to go back to school and to forget about Steel City. But I didn't want to go to university. They were sad about that. They were even sadder when I got my job at the factory.

'It *is* for the band,' I explained. 'Tom's guitar is broken. It was an accident, but I broke it. Now we have to get a new one. We're playing in the Battle of the Bands competition, and we can't have a guitarist without a guitar.'

Rachel didn't seem interested. 'Have you asked Mum and Dad?' she said.

'What do *you* think?' I answered. It was a silly question and Rachel knew it. Mum and Dad hated the band. I couldn't ask them for the money.

Rachel thought about this. Then she said, 'How many people in the world want to be pop stars?'

I didn't answer. I didn't have to – Rachel answered for me. 'Thousands of people do,' she said. 'And how many of them *become* pop stars?' She waited. 'Not very many.'

At last I said, 'This is really important, Rachel.'

Rachel gave me a long, sad look. Then she picked up her bag from the back of the chair. 'OK,' she said. 'How much do you want?'

◆

'Don't look so sad,' I told Tom the next day. 'Guess what's in my pocket.'

It was our lunch hour, and we were in the town centre. Tom

was still wearing his supermarket clothes. I took an envelope out of my pocket.

'What is it?' he asked.

'Money!' I said. 'There's enough to buy a guitar, I think. My sister lent it to me. To *us*.'

That great big smile was on Tom's face again. 'Really? That's great, Katy!'

He thought for a second. Then he said, 'Why are we waiting? Let's go to the music shop!'

We both ran to the music shop in the shopping centre. There were no customers. The only other person there was the owner. He was reading a music magazine.

Tom went straight to the guitars while I looked around the shop. I loved it here. When I looked at the pianos, I remembered all my years of piano lessons. My mum always wanted me to play Chopin and Beethoven. She wasn't very happy when I got the electric piano. She was even sadder when I started playing in Steel City.

I walked over to my boyfriend. Tom was really happy as he looked at all those guitars. He picked one up.

'Who am I?' he asked me. He closed his eyes and moved his fingers quickly over the guitar strings. The guitar wasn't plugged in so the sound was quiet.

'I don't know,' I laughed. 'Who are you?'

'Eric Clapton!' he said. Tom loved all the great guitar players.

Suddenly there was a cough from behind us. 'Can I help you?' asked the shop owner.

'Yes. How much is this guitar?' asked Tom.

When the shop owner told us, Tom's face became very white. I'm sure that my face did too.

'Er, that's a bit too expensive for us,' said Tom. 'Have you got anything that's cheaper?'

The shop owner showed us another guitar, and then another, and then another. There was just one small problem. We didn't have enough money. I had no idea that electric guitars were so expensive. I started to worry. What about the Battle of the Bands?

At last the shop owner asked Tom, 'How much money have you got?'

Tom told him. The man stood and thought for a minute. Then he said, 'Perhaps I can help you.'

He went into a room at the back of the shop. When he came out again, he was holding a guitar. A very old, very dirty guitar. 'It isn't beautiful, but it plays well,' he said. 'And it's cheap!'

Tom's face wasn't very happy, but he took the guitar.

'Let's go to another shop, Tom,' I said. But Tom didn't move. I looked at him. That guitar seemed really good there in his hands. I don't know why. Tom looked like a star. A great star!

Suddenly Tom smiled. I can't explain it, but it wasn't his usual nice smile. This smile was different. It was cold. For a second, I was afraid and I stepped back.

'Don't be silly!' I told myself. I looked again, and Tom's happy smile was back on his face. It went from ear to ear.

'I want this guitar, Katy,' he said.

♦

When I arrived home from work that night, I went straight to my room. I sat at my electric piano and started to write a new song. I usually wrote dance songs – fast and happy – but this one was different. It was a slow, sad song, and it came straight from my heart.

I never even looked at the clock. I worked at the piano for a long, long time. I wanted the music and words to be exactly right.

After I finished, I sat back. It was my best song, I knew that. But part of me was surprised by it, too. The song was so sad. It was easy to give it a name – 'A Last Goodbye'.

In my heart I was sure that this song was about Tom. The idea for it came to me in the music shop, when I saw him with that guitar.

But I still couldn't understand why the song was so sad. Tom and I were happy together. I was excited about the competition. I looked down at the song in my hands. Nothing was wrong in my life, was it? So why did I write this sad song?

Chapter 3   Trouble in the Band

The next day I was thinking about the competition again. I thought and dreamed about it all day at work. In my dreams Steel City always won the competition . . . But I told myself to stop dreaming. We had to start working hard. No band ever became famous without hard work. We planned to meet at Danny's house and practise that evening.

When we were all still at school, we practised every day. But life was different now. We all had jobs and we all finished work at different times of the day. It was difficult to find a time that was good for everyone. In fact, we could only practise two more times before the competition. It wasn't much. So at the end of the day I ran out of the factory. I didn't want to be late.

But something was wrong. Where was Tom? I looked up and down the street, but I couldn't see his car. The street was empty. I waited for twenty minutes, becoming more and more worried. Was he ill? Was he in trouble? I wanted to phone his house, but there was no telephone around. What should I do?

Suddenly I heard the noise of a bus. It was the number twenty-five. That bus went past Danny's house. I ran to the bus stop and jumped on the bus.

Thirty minutes later I was outside Danny's house. I knocked on the door. It opened and I was looking into our drummer's face. Aruna stood behind him. They were both angry.

'Where have you been?' asked Danny. 'We agreed to meet at half past six.'

'And where's Tom?' asked Aruna.

'I don't know,' I answered. 'He didn't pick me up outside the factory.'

'Tom isn't usually late, is he?' said Aruna.

'Never,' I said.

Now Aruna and Danny were worried too.

'Let's phone Tom's house,' I suggested. 'We can ask his parents where he is . . .'

Danny went to the phone. But suddenly we all heard a noise from outside. It was the sound of a car. It stopped, and a car door opened and closed.

Danny went to the front door. Tom was walking towards the house, carrying his new guitar in a case.

Aruna asked him the same question.

'Where have you been, Tom?'

'We were worried,' I added.

'I had things to do,' Tom said softly. He stepped into the house. He didn't even say sorry. He just opened his guitar case and said, 'Let's play.' Then he smiled, but it wasn't Tom's usual warm smile. This smile was thin and cold. That was the first strange thing about Tom that evening. But it wasn't the last.

'Which song shall we play first?' asked Aruna.

We were finally ready to practise. But it was late now and everyone was tired.

'How about "Electric Shoes"?' I suggested. It was one of our oldest songs, but it was still one of my favourites.

We started playing. After only a few seconds, it was clear that something was different. I couldn't believe my ears. It was Tom's guitar-playing. It was different and much, much better. It was great! I almost wanted to stop playing and just listen to him.

Aruna and Danny were surprised as well. When the song finished, Danny was smiling. He said, 'What happened, Tom?'

Tom didn't say anything. He just looked down at his new guitar. It looked much better now. It shone!

I was feeling good. With a wonderful guitarist, there was hope for Steel City in the competition. I was sure of it. I didn't ask why Tom's playing was suddenly so good.

'Yes, that was great, Tom,' said Aruna. 'You can come late next time too!'

We all laughed. All except Tom. He still didn't speak, but he gave Aruna a cold, dark look.

'It was just a joke, Tom,' she said nervously.

As I looked at Tom's face then, my happiness disappeared. Something was wrong. He seemed so different tonight.

'We have to play that song again,' said Tom. His voice was calm and quiet, but his eyes were angry.

'Why? I thought it was great!' said Danny.

'Me too,' said Aruna.

'And me,' I added.

'We have to play it again,' Tom repeated. Something about the sound of his voice made me afraid.

'Why, Tom?' I asked.

'Because it was terrible!' he suddenly shouted. 'All three of you were useless!' He pointed a finger at Danny. 'You were playing too fast,' he said.

'Wait a minute! I–' started Danny.

But now Tom was looking at Aruna. 'And your voice was terrible!' he said.

Then he turned to me. 'Your playing is OK, but it's boring. Put some life into it!'

We didn't know what to say. Why was Tom talking to us like this? What was wrong with him?

'Perhaps I should just leave?' I thought to myself.

At last Tom spoke again. 'We'll never win that competition if we don't practise more.' Then he put his head down and started to play the start of the song again.

I looked at Aruna and Danny. I knew what they were thinking. They were shocked and angry. But they were thinking about the competition too.

And so Danny started to drum. Then Aruna started playing. So I started playing too.

During the next two hours we practised most of our songs. And with each one, Tom's music became better and better. I almost forgot about that fight at the start of our practice.

But then another strange thing happened. After we finished our last song of the evening, we were all tired. But Tom didn't want to stop.

Danny stepped towards him. 'I don't know what's happened to you, Tom. You're playing wonderfully now,' he said. 'Can I look at your new guitar?'

Danny reached out for the guitar, but Tom pushed his hand away.

'What are you doing?' said Danny.

'Never touch my guitar,' said Tom angrily. 'Do you understand? Never.'

◆

Half an hour later I was sitting in Tom's car. He was driving me home. We didn't speak for a long time. I just looked out of the window. I was angry and confused.

'Why did you say that to Danny?' I said at last. 'He's a good friend.'

'I was trying to help the band,' answered Tom. Then he asked me, 'Do you really want to be a star, Katherine?'

Katherine? He usually called me Katy, not Katherine. What was wrong with him tonight?

'Yes,' I said quietly.

'People work hard to become stars. It doesn't matter if they're nice to their friends. If you don't want to work, you can forget all your dreams.'

Suddenly I remembered my new song from the night before. I pulled it out of my pocket.

'I *do* want to be a star,' I said. 'And this is going to help us. I think it's the best song that I've ever written, Tom.'

He took the song from my hand and started to look at it. He continued driving with one hand on the wheel.

'Don't read it now!' I shouted. 'You can look at it later. Watch the road!'

Tom pushed the paper into his shirt pocket. He said nothing. He was driving very fast now.

'Please don't go so fast,' I said. 'It's dangerous.'

Tom went more slowly for a few minutes, but he soon started to drive faster and faster again.

'Drive more slowly!' I shouted. 'What's wrong with you? You've been really strange all night. And why can't anyone touch that new guitar?'

I turned around and reached for the guitar on the back seat. There was a terrible sound as Tom suddenly stopped the car.

His eyes were grey and cold. 'Don't go near my guitar,' he said. 'It's very special to me.'

We didn't speak for the rest of the way home. I had a lot to think about. What was wrong with Tom? Why was he so angry?

And why was he playing so well now? Why? Why? Why? I had a lot of questions, but no answers.

When we reached my house, I got out of the car. Tom didn't say goodnight. He just drove away very fast.

'Something very strange is happening,' I thought. And it all started when Tom bought that guitar.

Chapter 4   The Promise

I couldn't stop thinking about it. Something was wrong – very, very wrong. I thought about it all through the next two days. What was the problem? Why could Tom play so well with his new guitar? And why was he so angry? I had to talk to someone about it. On Saturday I decided to phone Aruna.

'He's probably worried about the competition,' she said.

I wasn't sure. 'Maybe,' I said. 'But why can he suddenly play so well?'

Aruna laughed. 'It doesn't matter! I'm just happy that he's playing better! I think we can even win the competition now.'

After I put the phone down, I could still hear Aruna's words: 'we can even win the competition now...' It was true, but it didn't answer my question.

'What are you waiting for?' I asked myself. 'You want to know what's happening to Tom? So go to his house and find out.'

Half an hour later I knocked on the door of Tom's house. His mum opened the door. Usually she was a happy person and her smile was as big and friendly as her son's. But today she wasn't smiling.

'Hello, Mrs Webster,' I said.

'Tom isn't here,' she said. 'But come in, Katherine. Would you like a coffee?'

'Yes, please.' I stepped inside.

Tom's mum started to say something, but then she stopped. She seemed worried.

'Is something wrong?' I asked her.

'It's Tom,' she said. 'He just sits in his room all day and plays that guitar. An hour ago his boss at the supermarket telephoned. He wanted to know where Tom was.'

'What did you do?'

'I sent Tom to work, of course. But it wasn't easy.' Mrs Webster looked at me. 'What's wrong with him, Katherine?'

'I don't know,' I said.

I had an idea. Perhaps it was good that Tom wasn't around. I wanted to have a look at that guitar.

'Mrs Webster, can I go and get something from Tom's room?' I asked. 'I gave him a new song on Wednesday and now I'd like to work on it.'

'Of course you can,' she said.

I didn't like telling her a lie. But I was doing it for Tom. I ran up the stairs and opened the door to his room. There were clothes and CDs all over the floor.

I looked around. There were some pieces of paper on Tom's desk. I looked through them. My song was there. I picked it up and put it in my pocket. Now I wasn't completely lying to Tom's mum.

Suddenly the hairs on the back of my neck stood up.

Someone was watching me. I could feel it. Someone in the room! I turned round quickly. But there was nobody there.

Then I noticed the guitar. It was in the corner of the room next to an amplifier. I can't explain it, but that guitar seemed to be watching me.

I told myself to stop being silly. This was real life, not a film! Slowly I stepped towards the guitar, and I plugged it in. I'm not sure why I did it. I pressed the switch on the amplifier and saw the little red ON light.

Slowly I moved my fingers across the guitar strings. Nothing. There was no sound.

I looked at the amplifier. It was plugged in. But no noise came out. I turned the sound up from three to five. Then I tried the guitar again. Still nothing.

A sudden fear filled my heart. I ran out of the room and down the stairs. At the bottom, I stopped. Why was I being so silly? But then I heard a noise from upstairs. It was coming from inside Tom's room.

Was I imagining it? Or was that the soft sound of a guitar?

♦

An hour later I was back inside the music shop. Again, I was the only customer in there. The shop owner was standing and reading a music magazine.

'Excuse me,' I said. He looked up slowly. 'I was in here a few days ago. My boyfriend bought a guitar.'

'Yes?' said the shop owner. He didn't seem to remember me or Tom.

I continued, 'It was an old guitar. You got it from the back of the shop.'

'Ah, yes,' said the shop owner. 'I remember. But how can I help you now?'

'I need to know more about that guitar,' I said. 'Where did it come from?'

The shop owner thought for a minute. 'That old guitar has been around in the back of the shop for a long time.' He started to look through some piles of paper behind his desk. Soon there were papers everywhere.

At last he waved a piece of paper in the air. 'Here it is! Yes, I remember now. A woman came in with that guitar about six months ago. She didn't want much money for it. She didn't want it in her house. That's what she said.'

'Could you give me her name and address?'

'Why not?' said the shop owner. He wrote a name and address on a piece of paper and gave it to me. The name was Linda Carter, and the address was for a flat in Gresham Street, on the other side of town.

'Thanks,' I said. I turned to leave.

'Wait!' shouted the shop owner. 'I've just thought of something.'

'What?'

'I remember why that guitar was so cheap. The woman was sure that . . . it brought bad luck.'

After I left, those words came back to me: 'bad luck'.

♦

It was dark when I arrived in Gresham Street. It was raining too. I hurried through the entrance to the flats. Linda Carter lived on the tenth floor. The lift was broken, so I had to climb the stairs. When I reached the tenth floor, I was hot and tired. I knocked on the door of Linda Carter's flat.

I had to wait a long time before the door opened. A woman's thin face looked into mine. She was about forty years old. The door wasn't open very wide, but I could see a little of the room behind her. There was a big man sitting on the sofa. He was watching an old rock band on television. He didn't move.

'Are you Linda Carter?' I asked the woman.

'Yes. What do you want?'

'My name's Katherine,' I said. 'I'd like to ask you a few questions. My boyfriend has bought the guitar which you–'

When she heard the word 'guitar', the woman's face turned white.

'Shhh! Be quiet!' she said quickly. She looked nervously at the man inside. Then she pushed me back. She stepped outside and closed the door behind her.

'My husband has finally stopped thinking about that guitar,' she said. 'He's stopped having bad dreams about it. I don't want them to start again now.'

It was clear that she wanted her husband to be safe. But safe from what?

'I'll go away, Mrs Carter,' I said. 'But first I want to know more about that guitar.'

Linda Carter didn't say anything.

'Something's wrong with my boyfriend. And it started when he got that guitar.'

I waited. She was thinking about it.

At last she said softly, 'OK. I'll tell you. But you must promise that you'll go away then. Go away and never come back here.'

I saw something in her eyes then. It was fear.

'I promise,' I said.

Chapter 5   Linda Carter's Story

'It happened twenty years ago,' said Linda Carter. 'I was working as a waitress, but I had big dreams. My boyfriend Phil played bass guitar in a band.

'The band was called Circle of Gold. They were really good. But they were only good because of the guitarist. His name was David Ryan, and he was special. He wrote all their songs. But his guitar music was best of all. He played wonderfully.'

Linda stopped. She was remembering the sound of that guitar.

'But music was the only important thing for David,' she continued. 'He sat at home and practised all day. He even lost his job because he never arrived at work at the right time. He wasn't worried. He wanted to be a star.'

'And the others in the band?' I asked.

'In David's opinion, they were all lazy,' she said. 'He shouted at them after gigs. He told them to practise more and more. He wanted them to practise all the time.'

'Why didn't Phil leave?' I asked.

'Nobody left,' answered Linda. 'They all wanted to be stars, too.'

'So what happened?'

'There was a big competition,' said Linda. I suddenly felt afraid.

'It was on 10th July, 1980,' she said. The fear in my heart grew – that was the same date as the Battle of the Bands competition *this* year.

'It was the last time that Circle of Gold ever played,' she continued. 'They were good, but David wasn't happy. After the concert he screamed at the band. He was really angry. Then he drove away alone. Nobody ever saw him again.'

'Why not?' I asked.

There were tears in Linda's eyes now. 'He had a car crash,' she said. 'He died immediately. He was driving too fast, and the road was wet . . .' She stopped. 'After that, the band stopped playing. It was impossible without David. He was the heart of that band.'

'What happened to you and Phil?'

'I married him,' she said. 'He doesn't play in a band now. He's a lorry driver . . . and I'm still a waitress.'

So Phil was the man in the flat. I was almost afraid to ask the next question. 'And David Ryan's guitar?'

There was a cold look in Linda's eyes. 'The guitar didn't break in the crash,' she explained. 'David's parents didn't want it, so Phil asked for it. He wanted to remember his time with the band.'

'Did it help?'

'He lived in the past because of that guitar. For years he had bad dreams about David and the crash. But still he wanted to keep the guitar. And then, about a year ago, strange things started to happen.'

'What strange things?'

'His dreams became worse. But that wasn't the only thing . . . Sometimes I could hear that guitar. But when I went into the room, nobody was ever there. Nobody! Perhaps I imagined it. But I was afraid and I sold the guitar. Phil was angry. But I didn't tell him where it was. That was last year. He's just beginning to forget about it. So go now, before you bring the bad dreams back.'

'Wait!' I said. 'Tell me more about David Ryan. It's–'

Suddenly there was a deep voice from inside the flat.

'Linda? Who's there?' It was Phil, Linda's husband.

'Nobody,' shouted Linda. 'Someone's trying to sell something.'

She turned to me. 'I've told you what happened. Believe it or not, but never come here again.'

She disappeared into the flat.

Outside it was still raining. I needed to talk to somebody. Aruna was busy – she worked in a video shop at the weekends. Danny was never at home, so I couldn't tell him. Who could I tell?

Suddenly I knew. I ran all the way to the bus stop.

◆

'Come in,' said Rachel.

My sister was sitting on her bed and writing a letter. I was surprised that she wasn't studying.

'Can I ask you something, Rachel?' I began.

My sister looked up slowly. 'OK.'

'Do you believe in ghosts?'

I felt silly, but Rachel didn't laugh.

'I love history,' she said. 'And history is full of ghosts. I don't believe in ghosts who walk around old houses at midnight. But I *do* believe that the past is important. It touches all our lives.' She looked into my eyes. 'Why?'

I started to tell her. 'It all began when you lent me the money for Tom's guitar . . .'

Again, Rachel surprised me. She listened carefully.

Twenty minutes later, I finished my story.

Rachel thought about it all. Then she asked, 'When's your next practice?'

'Wednesday, at Danny's house,' I answered. 'It's our last one before the competition. Why?'

'I'd like to see Tom before I give you my opinion. I'll come to your practice too,' she said.

♦

Danny and Aruna were surprised to see Rachel with me at the next practice. In the kitchen Aruna said to me, 'Doesn't Rachel hate pop music? What's she doing here?'

'She needs a rest from her studies,' I answered.

When we joined the others, Aruna looked at her watch.

'It's twenty to seven,' she said. 'He's late again.'

I was feeling nervous but I tried to hide it.

We waited for ten more minutes. No Tom. But then there was a knock at the door. 'He's here!' Danny shouted to us. I looked at Rachel.

When Tom came into the room, I was shocked. His face was white, and his hair was long and dirty. It hung round his face. His clothes were different too: he was wearing an old T-shirt, a pair of jeans and dark glasses. Of course, he was carrying *that* guitar.

Rachel saw that I was surprised. But Danny was going to his drums. 'Let's start!' he said. 'First we have to choose our songs for the competition. Each band can only play two songs.'

The others started talking about our songs. I couldn't stop thinking about my new song. But it was too late for the band to learn a new song. I didn't say anything while the others talked. At last they chose two songs.

We played each song three times. It was difficult for me to play that night. I was thinking about too many other things. I really wanted Rachel to believe me.

We were still playing when the telephone rang. Danny went to answer it.

'It's for you, Tom,' he shouted from the next room.

When Tom left, I went to my sister.

'What do you think?' I asked.

'I think the music's terrible,' answered Rachel.

'No, about Tom.'

'I don't know,' she said. 'I haven't seen him for a long time, but he seems different. He's a much better guitarist now. But I don't–'

Rachel stopped. There were shouts from the next room.

'Good! Do you think I'm interested in that boring job? I've finished with it . . .'

We all stood and listened.

'Who's he talking to?' I asked.

'His boss,' said Danny. 'He called Tom's house and Tom's mum gave him my number. He says that Tom hasn't come to work twice now.'

'I don't need your job!' shouted Tom from the next room. 'Circle of Gold are going to be big. I'm going to be a star! What do you think about that?'

Tom threw the phone down and came back into the room. Nobody knew what to say.

At last, Tom spoke. 'OK,' he said calmly. 'Let's play each song one more time.'

24

Chapter 6   An Old Newspaper

Tom left first at the end of our practice. He didn't speak. He didn't even say goodbye. He just left with his guitar. A few seconds later we heard him drive away fast.

Rachel and I left next. I was afraid that my sister didn't believe me about Tom.

When we were outside, I said, 'I don't understand it. He wasn't so angry with the band tonight. But last week he was terrible. You must believe me. Something's wrong.'

Rachel held up one hand. 'OK, OK. I *do* believe you.'

'You do?'

'Yes,' answered Rachel. 'Didn't you hear what Tom said on the telephone to his boss? "Circle of Gold are going to be big." That's what he said.'

My heart was going faster and faster. Circle of Gold was the name of David Ryan's band twenty years ago.

'What can we do?' I asked.

'I think we need more information about all of this,' said my sister. 'And I know the best place to find it.'

'Where?'

'The library, of course!'

♦

I met Rachel outside the library after work the next day.

'I haven't been here for a long time,' I said. 'It all seems very different.'

'They had to build part of it again a few years ago after a fire.' My sister looked at me. 'So you haven't been here for years?' she asked.

I didn't answer. I knew that Rachel came here a few times a week. It was almost a second home to her. I looked around. I didn't know where to go.

'We need the second floor,' Rachel said. 'They keep all the old newspapers there.' She walked towards the lift, and I followed her.

On the second floor Rachel went to the information desk.

'Excuse me,' she said. 'We're looking for an old copy of the town newspaper.'

'Which one do you want?' asked the librarian.

'The eleventh of July, 1980,' I said. The day after the competition. It wasn't difficult to remember the date. This year's competition was also on 10th July.

'I don't know about that,' said the librarian. 'We had a fire here a few years ago, you know. We saved most of the newspapers. But a lot of the older ones were burned.'

'Could you look, please?' asked Rachel.

The woman left. I looked around at all the books. There were only a few other people in this part of the library. They were sitting at desks with their heads down and their books open. 'Boring!' I thought. But I knew that this place wasn't boring to Rachel.

'You like this place, don't you?' I asked her.

Rachel smiled. 'I love it.'

'But why?' I really wanted to understand.

'How do you feel when you play in the band?' asked Rachel.

'Great,' I answered.

'And I feel great when I'm studying here. I'm good at it and I like doing it. I enjoy learning things . . . things about the past.'

The librarian came back. She put something on the desk in front of us.

'Here it is,' she said. 'At least, here's part of it.'

We looked down at the paper. Parts of it were yellow, and parts were brown. Other parts were completely gone.

'After the fire, we threw a lot of newspapers away,' explained the librarian sadly. 'We decided to keep the ones that you could read a little.'

Rachel carefully picked the newspaper up and we took it to one of the tables. Slowly Rachel started to turn the pages. Some of them were almost impossible to read because of the fire.

'Here it is!' said Rachel suddenly.

I looked down at the page. It was very hard to read. I saw the words 'Music News' at the top of the page. Under this, it said: 'Great Night At Music Competition'.

We couldn't read the rest of the news story. But there were also three photographs on the page. Each one was a photo of a band in concert.

'What are these people all doing now, twenty years later?' asked Rachel. 'They probably work in offices and banks.'

'I know what one of these people is doing now,' I said. My finger moved to the smiling face of a bass guitarist. He was much younger and thinner in the photo, but I knew his face. 'He's called Phil Carter. He's a lorry driver.'

I read the words under the photograph: 'Circle of Gold'. Ryan's band was in the newspaper! So they didn't win that night, but they were second or third. They *almost* won. But 'almost' wasn't enough for David Ryan.

I felt suddenly afraid. It wasn't because of Phil Carter. No, it was the guitarist next to him in the photo. He was looking straight into the camera with cold grey eyes. His face was thin and white and his hair was long. He wore a white T-shirt, a pair of jeans and an old jacket. In his hands was a guitar – *that* guitar.

I suddenly felt cold. I was looking at David Ryan. But when was the photograph taken? On the night of the competition? Perhaps it was taken just minutes before the band lost. Just minutes before David angrily drove away for the last time ever.

'Hey!' said Rachel. She was shocked. 'He looks exactly like Tom!'

It was true. We were looking at a photograph from twenty years ago. But the guitarist in the photograph looked like Tom at our practice that evening.

♦

On the bus home, I looked at the streets outside the window. 'What are we going to do now?' I asked myself. I still couldn't really believe what was happening.

At last I spoke. 'It's all true, isn't it, Rachel? David Ryan has come back. He's a . . .'

My sister said the word for me. 'A ghost. Yes, I think so.'

'But how can this happen?'

'Who knows?' said Rachel. Her eyes were wide. 'I've read about things like this. I never believed them until now.' She thought for a second. 'Some part of David Ryan didn't die in that crash twenty years ago. I think that his ghost is trying to come back. And the way back into our world is through the most important thing that he ever owned – his guitar.'

Part of me still couldn't believe it. This was real life! But another, deeper part of me really believed it all. It was true!

'But Tom?' I asked. 'Does he understand what's happening?' There were tears in my eyes. I was thinking about all my happy times with Tom.

'He's probably confused,' said Rachel. 'I think that Tom Webster and the ghost of David Ryan are fighting inside one person. They probably don't understand what's happening.'

A terrible idea hit me. 'Wait a minute,' I said. 'David Ryan lost his job twenty years ago, and yesterday Tom lost his job at the supermarket. David Ryan's band played in a competition, and now we're going to play in one. What if–?' I was thinking about the car crash, but I was afraid to say the words.

Rachel thought about this. Her face became very white. 'You're right,' she said. 'History sometimes repeats itself. I've learned that from my studies.' She thought for a minute. 'If your band loses in the competition, Tom will probably do the same as David Ryan.'

My hands started shaking.

'You mean he'll . . . die?'

'Not if we change things,' said Rachel. Her voice was shaking, too. 'The concert has to be different this time. If your band doesn't play, then there won't be an accident.'

I thought fast. 'But even if I don't play, the others will. I can't stop them. This is too important to them.'

'You can take Tom's guitar,' suggested Rachel. 'He can't play without it. History won't repeat itself. The crash won't happen.'

'We can't go near the guitar,' I said. 'He keeps it with him all the time.'

We both thought for a long time. Was there any hope? I was starting to think that there wasn't.

But then Rachel said, 'I've got another idea. David Ryan was angry because his band lost the competition, wasn't he? So he drove off too fast.'

'Yes?'

'So, it's easy. Steel City has to *win* that competition. That will change everything! Maybe the ghost of David Ryan will disappear if his band wins this time.'

Chapter 7   The Battle of the Bands

The big night came at last – the night of the competition. All the bands had to arrive at the City Arena early. I went with Danny and Aruna in Danny's van. We carried our things inside. The place was very busy. We all had to wait in a big room behind the stage. Of course, Tom arrived late. He didn't speak to any of us. He didn't even look at us. What was happening inside his head now? When I looked at him, I felt a terrible fear. Not fear for myself . . . fear for him.

Of course, that guitar never left his hands. I was starting to hate it. But I told myself to be calm. To save Tom, we had to win the competition.

At about seven o'clock, the crowd started to arrive at the arena. We couldn't see them, but we could hear them. There were a lot of people there.

An hour later someone from the radio station walked on to the stage. Her name was Lisa Jones and she was famous (in our area!). It was her job to introduce all the bands. She picked up the microphone.

'Welcome to the Battle of the Bands!' she shouted.

The crowd cheered. Then she introduced the judges. One of

them was from the 'Top Twenty' music programme. Another was an actor from our town. I didn't know his name but I knew his face from TV. The third judge was from a big record company.

On stage, Lisa Jones said, 'Our judges will have a difficult decision tonight. It's an important decision too, because only one band can win. And now here is the first band of the evening... the Tigers of the Mind!'

The crowd cheered again, and the first band started to play. They were OK, but I didn't listen much. I was looking for Rachel. Where was she?

The second band went on stage. They were terrible. They were young and nervous, and they made a lot of mistakes. I was starting to feel more hopeful. But then the third band – The Passengers – played. Their songs were great – fast and exciting. You couldn't stop your feet moving. As I listened, I started to worry more and more. We had to win! But could we? And if we didn't win... I looked at Tom.

We listened to three more bands. Then it was time for us. I could hear my own heart, as Lisa Jones introduced us.

'And now, please give a big welcome to... Steel City!'

The crowd clapped politely as we walked out on to the stage. I was surprised to see so many people. It was our biggest crowd. I was nervous, but I told myself, 'Don't think about the crowd. Don't think about ghosts or car crashes. Don't worry about Rachel. Just play! Play better than you've ever played before!'

'One, two, three, four!' counted Danny. We started our first song. Immediately, I forgot my worries. Everyone played their best. Aruna, Danny, me... and, of course, Tom. His guitar-playing that night was wonderful. Better than wonderful! The crowd loved it too. Some of them stood up and started to dance. At the end of our first song there was a big cheer.

Our second song was even better. And again Tom's guitar was really special. But Tom didn't seem happy. He looked down as he played. At the end of the song, the crowd clapped and cheered wildly.

'That was wonderful!' said Aruna as we left the stage.

'We're going to win,' said Danny with a big smile on his face.

'What do you think, Tom?' I asked.

But our guitarist didn't answer. I wanted him to take those dark glasses off. I wanted to look into his eyes. He seemed angry again, but why?

There were three more bands after us. They seemed to play for hours. I couldn't rest until we won. I wanted Tom – my Tom – to be safe again.

Finally the last band played their last song. The judges had to make their decision now. The crowd waited. The bands behind the stage waited. Five minutes passed, then ten minutes, but still nothing happened.

I couldn't sit. I was so nervous. I walked to the side of the stage. What were the judges doing? At last Lisa Jones walked back to the microphone.

'The judges have not been able to make a decision,' she said. 'They couldn't choose between two of the bands ... The Passengers and Steel City.' The crowd cheered for each band.

'This has only ever happened once before,' she continued. 'So this is what we're going to do. Both bands will come back on stage and play one more song. Then the judges will choose a winner.'

What? We had to play again? This was terrible! I was afraid to play again. The other band was really good. I wasn't sure that we could win against them. My hands started to shake with fear.

The Passengers went out on stage. I didn't know what to do. I couldn't think. Suddenly a hand fell on my arm. I turned around. It was Rachel! But she wasn't alone. Phil Carter was with her. He seemed confused.

'Rachel, where have you been?' I asked.

My sister's face was white with worry. 'I was coming to the arena when I had an idea,' she explained. 'I was thinking about that newspaper story – the one from twenty years ago. I was nervous because we didn't see the complete story. I hate not having all the information. I remembered what you said about Mr Carter. So I went to his flat. At first his wife didn't want me to talk to him, but I refused to go away. Finally she agreed.' Rachel turned to the big man next to her, 'Mr Carter, tell Katherine about that night twenty years ago.'

'It was great at first,' said Phil. 'Our band played really well. We were the best band there. Of course, we won.'

Won? My blood froze. 'But . . . you lost, didn't you? That's why David Ryan was angry. That's why he drove off too fast . . .'

'No,' said Phil Carter sadly. 'We *won* the competition that night. But David still wasn't happy. That was his problem – he was never happy. After all the bands finished, the judges couldn't choose between Circle of Gold and one other band. Both bands had to play one more song. We were ready to play, but David started shouting at us. He was angry about all our mistakes. He didn't want us to play again that night.'

'So what happened?' I asked.

'We had a big fight. David went on stage and played our last song alone. I was angry with him, but he played that last song wonderfully. So Circle of Gold won – but David was still angry. That's why he drove away alone. That's why he had that terrible accident.'

I was trying to understand all of this. 'So our plan is useless,' I said to Rachel. 'If we win the competition, nothing will change. It will be the same as twenty years ago.'

'I think so,' said Rachel with tears in her eyes. 'I'm sorry, but we were wrong. If you win the competition, something terrible will happen. Or . . .'

'Or we can try to lose,' I said.

But was I too late already? The Passengers were finishing their song. It was time for Steel City to play.

Chapter 8   The Last Goodbye

I had to think fast. My first idea was this: refuse to play. Don't even go on to the stage.

No, that plan was too dangerous. The band didn't need my electric piano. And they all really wanted to play and win.

I was still thinking about it when Tom walked out on to the

stage alone. He plugged in his guitar.

What was happening? Aruna and Danny were standing behind the stage. I ran to them quickly.

'What's wrong?' I asked. 'Why aren't you on the stage too?'

They both seemed unhappy and confused.

'Tom says that there's a new plan,' said Aruna.

'He says that you agreed to it,' added Danny.

'Agreed to what?' I asked.

'He's playing the last song alone.'

I almost screamed. Like David Ryan twenty years ago, Tom wanted to play alone. History was repeating itself. I was frozen with fear.

On stage Tom started to play. I can't find the words to describe that music. It was great. Wonderful. It was beautiful.

When Tom started to sing, I knew the song. It was my new one, 'A Last Goodbye'. It was a good song, but tonight it was really special.

The crowd agreed. They were watching something wonderful. Part of me was really pleased that my song was so popular. *My* song! But another part of me was screaming: 'Do something, or Tom is going to die! Don't fail now!'

But do what?

Suddenly I knew. I ran out into the bright lights of the stage. I tried not to look at the crowd. I moved behind Tom and pushed him hard. He reached out to the microphone, and fell with it to the floor. I pulled the guitar away from him.

The crowd started to shout angrily. I told myself not to think about them. This was too important. I held the guitar over my head and I brought it down hard. There was a terrible sound as it hit the floor. I did it again, then again.

People in the crowd were holding their hands over their ears now. It didn't matter. I didn't think about anything. I just wanted to break that guitar into a thousand pieces. Finally I pushed it into

one of the big speakers on the stage. The guitar gave a final scream. Then nothing. I dropped the broken pieces on to the floor.

The guitar was gone. The crowd were silent. There was no sound in the arena. I could hear the drumming of my own heart.

Tom was standing again now. He took a step towards me. I stepped back nervously. But he just smiled and took off his dark glasses. I looked into those grey eyes. I wasn't looking at Tom. I was looking at the ghost of David Ryan. Don't ask me how I knew this. I just knew it in my heart. But something was different about him now. For the first time, he seemed to understand what was happening.

'I'm never going to be a big star, am I?' he said. He was still smiling, but it was a sad smile.

I couldn't lie to him. 'No.'

'It was a beautiful song,' he said. I knew he was talking about my song.

'Thanks,' I said. 'You played it beautifully.' I looked into those grey eyes without fear now. No fear, just sadness.

I took a step towards him and kissed his face. 'Goodbye, David,' I said.

The guitarist smiled one last time. Then his head fell to his chest. A few seconds later his eyes opened again. I looked into them. Then I knew that David Ryan was gone. Perhaps the eyes were bluer now. Perhaps the smile was wider. But this was Tom. I knew it in my heart. My boyfriend was back! I threw my arms around him.

Tom caught me. 'Er . . . what's happening, Katy?' he asked.

Katy! He called me Katy! I almost cried with happiness.

'And what happened to my guitar?' said Tom.

Of course, Steel City didn't win that night. It didn't matter. It didn't seem important now. The Passengers were a really good band. In fact, they made their first CD a few months after the competition and I bought it. I hope that they'll be big stars.

And me? I'm still working in the factory, but I'm going to leave at the end of the summer. I've decided to go to college. Don't worry – I still play in Steel City. But it's good to have more than one plan. You never know what will happen in life.

The band is doing well. We haven't made our first CD yet, but we will one day. I don't just dream and dream all day about becoming a big pop star now. But I'm still sure that I want to be a musician. Sometimes I lose hope, but then I think of David Ryan. I remember how he played my song that night.

There's one last thing to tell you. It happened soon after the Battle of the Bands. I was walking past Rachel's room. Suddenly I stopped. I couldn't believe my ears. Pop music! Rachel was listening to pop music in her room.

I opened the door. 'What's that?' I asked. In fact, I knew the song. It was one of my favourites.

Rachel turned the radio off quickly.

'I thought you hated pop music,' I said with a big smile.

Rachel's face was red. 'I *did* hate it,' she said. 'But at the Battle of the Bands competition, I changed my mind. When you broke that guitar on stage, it was really. . . exciting. I can't explain it.'

I started to laugh, then Rachel laughed too. I turned the radio on again and we both listened to the end of the song.

ACTIVITIES

Chapter 1

Before you read

1 Imagine that you are starting a band. Discuss what equipment you and the other musicians will need. Look at the Word List at the back of the book and use words from the list in your discussion.

2 Read the Introduction to the book and discuss these questions. What do you think?

    a What is the secret of Tom's new guitar?

    b What does Katy want to save Tom from?

    c How can she save him?

While you read

3 Answer the questions.

    a Who is telling the story? ....

    b Where does she work? ....

    c What does she really want to be? ....

    d What is Steel City? ....

    e What does Tom play in the band? ....

    f Where do the band have a gig? ....

    g Who is the singer in the band? ....

    h What does Danny play? ....

    i Do the people in the pub cheer the band? ....

    j What is the name of the band competition? ....

    k What happens to Tom's guitar? ....

After you read

4 How does Katy feel about:

    a her job?   **c** Tom?

    b Steel City?   **d** Tom's guitar playing?

5 Work in pairs and have this conversation.

Student A: You are Katy. Tell a friend about the Battle of the Bands. Explain the competition. How did Steel City win a place in it? Say how you feel about it.

Student B: You are a friend at Katy's factory. Ask her questions about her band and the competition.

Chapters 2–3

Before you read

6 Look at the titles of the next two chapters:

'The New Guitar'　　　'Trouble in the Band'

Guess the answer to these questions. Then read the chapters and check your answers.

a How will the band get the money for a new guitar?

b Where will they get the guitar?

c What kind of trouble in the band will there be?

While you read

7 Are these sentences right (✓) or wrong (✗)?

a Katy's sister doesn't like pop music. .....

b Katy's mother lends her money. .....

c Tom buys the most expensive guitar in the music shop. .....

d Katy always writes sad songs. .....

e She writes a song about Tom. .....

f Katy goes to the next practice by car. .....

g Tom arrives late for the practice. .....

h Tom's guitar playing is better. .....

i Tom seems like another person. .....

j Katy goes home from the practice by bus. .....

k Katy gives Tom her new song. .....

l Katy is worried about the new guitar. .....

After you read

8 How does Tom change after he has bought the guitar? Discuss your thoughts with another student.

9 Write some words for Katy's song, 'The Last Goodbye'.

Chapters 4–5

Before you read

10 In the next chapters Katy learns more about the history of Tom's guitar. Guess the answer to these questions. Then read and check your answers.

    a Who owned the guitar before it was sold to Tom?

    b Why did the guitar go to the music shop?

While you read

11 Put these sentences in the correct order, 1–11.

    a Katy goes to Linda Carter's flat. .....

    b Katy goes to Tom's house. .....

    c Tom leaves his job at the supermarket. .....

    d Rachel agrees to help her sister. .....

    e Katy tries to play Tom's guitar. .....

    f The man in the music shop gives Katy the address of the guitar's old owner. .....

    g Katy takes her song from Tom's room. .....

    h The band meet to practice again. .....

    i Linda Carter tells the story of her husband's old band. .....

    j Katy talks to Aruna. .....

    k Tom's mother tells Katy that she is worried. .....

After you read

12 Complete Linda Carter's story.

    'My husband Phil played in a … called Circle of Gold. David Ryan played the … and he … all the band's songs. One night they were playing in a big … . After the concert, David Ryan was very … . He … away in his car. He went too … and the road was … . He had a terrible … . He … immediately.'

13 Who says these words. Who to and why?

    a 'She didn't want it in her house.'

    b 'I promise.'

    c 'Go now before you bring the bad dreams back.'

    d 'Do you believe in ghosts?'

    e 'I love history.'

    f 'I'm going to be a star!'

Chapter 6

Before you read

14 Discuss these questions.

  a Do you think that Rachel believes Katy now? Why (not)?

  b In the next chapter Katy and Rachel go to the library. What are they looking for? Will they find it?

While you read

15 Who is it? Write the names.

  a He leaves the practice without saying goodbye. ....

  b He had a band called 'Circle of Gold'. ....

  c She suggests a visit to the library. ....

  d He was in Circle of Gold and now drives lorries. ....

  e He looked the way Tom looks now. ....

  f His ghost is in the guitar. ....

  g She says that Steel City must win the Battle of the Bands. ....

After you read

16 Discuss these questions.

  a Who says, 'History sometimes repeats itself'? What does this mean? Why is this idea important in the story?

  b What are the main differences between Katy and Rachel? How does Chapter 6 show these differences?

Chapters 7–8

Before you read

17 Discuss these questions.

  a Will Rachel's plan work?

  b What do you think will happen at the Battle of the Bands?

  c How will the story end?

18 There is a mistake in each sentence. Circle it and write the correct words.

    a Aruna arrives late for the competition. ....

    b Tom's guitar-playing in the competition is terrible. ....

    c Tom seems unhappy after the band's first song. ....

    d The judges can't decide between three of the bands. ....

    e Rachel arrives with Linda Carter. ....

    f Katy learns that Circle of Gold lost the competition twenty years ago. ....

    g Tom plays the last song alone on the piano. ....

    h The crowd cheer after Katy breaks the guitar. ....

    i Katy knows that Phil Carter's ghost has left her boyfriend. ....

    j After the competition, Rachel starts to play in a pop band, too. ....

After you read

19 Compare your ending to the story to the real ending. Which one do you prefer? Why?

20 Work in pairs and have this imaginary conversation.

    Student A: You are David Ryan's ghost. Give a last message to Katy before you disappear.

    Student B: You are Katy. Listen to the ghost. What do you want to tell him?

Writing

21 Imagine that you are a person in the book (not Katy). Tell the story as you understood it.

22 Imagine that you are a reporter for a local newspaper. Write about what happened at the Battle of the Bands competition.

23 You are making a film of this story. Choose actors to play Katy, Tom and Rachel. Write notes for the actors to explain your ideas about these people.

24 Choose part of the story. Think about how it will look in your film. Describe the place, and people's actions. What will they say? Remember that you can change the words in the book.

25 It is ten years after the Battle of the Bands, and Steel City is a successful band. Write a magazine story. In it, Katy describes the life and history of the band.

26 Write a short report about the book for students to read on the Internet. Say what it is about (but don't tell the ending!).

27 Talk to some other students about their favourite kinds of music. Write a newspaper report about what you discover.

28 Write another ghost story. Your ghost can be in something different – but something that people use every day.

Answers for the Activities in this book are available from the Pearson English Readers website. A free Activity Worksheet is also available from the website. Activity worksheets are part of the Pearson English Readers Teacher Support Programme, which also includes Progress tests and Graded Reader Guidelines. For more information, please visit: www.pearsonenglishreaders.com